A PICTORIAL HISTORY OF COSTUME

ILLUSTRIERTE KOSTÜMGESCHICHTE
HISTOIRE ILLUSTRÉE DU COSTUME
STORIA ILLUSTRATA DEL COSTUME
HISTORIA ILUSTRADA DEL VESTIDO
絵で見る服装史
服装史畫冊

A PICTORIAL HISTORY OF COSTUME

ILLUSTRIERTE KOSTÜMGESCHICHTE
HISTOIRE ILLUSTRÉE DU COSTUME
STORIA ILLUSTRATA DEL COSTUME
HISTORIA ILUSTRADA DEL VESTIDO
絵で見る服装史
服装史畫冊

THE PEPIN PRESS

First published in 1998 by The Pepin Press

Edited and produced by Dorine van den Beukel

ISBN 90 5496 046 9

The Pepin Press
POB 10349 • 1001 EH Amsterdam • The Netherlands
Tel (+) 31 20 4202021 • Fax (+) 31 20 4201152 • E-Mail pepin@euronet.nl

Printed in Singapore

A pictorial history of costume

The five hundred colour illustrations in this book date from the nineteenth century. They show the attire of people in various parts of the world at different points in history. The handcoloured engravings present costumes dating from the Stone Age until well into the nineteenth century. This collection includes attire from Ancient Egypt, the Middle East, Russia and most European countries, showing the differences between regions, classes – royalty, civilians, military, nobility, clergy – and fashions. The historical costumes of many Asian countries, including Persia, India, Burma, Thailand, Malaya, Indonesia, China and Japan, are also depicted.

Descriptions of the illustrations can be found from page 209.

Illustrierte Kostümgeschichte

Die 500 Farbillustrationen in diesem Buch stammen aus dem 19. Jahrhundert und zeigen Kleider, Trachten und Kostüme aus unterschiedlichen Teilen der Welt und verschiedenen Geschichtsepochen. Die Trachten auf den hand-kolorierten Stichen stammen aus Epochen, die von der Steinzeit bis weit in das 19. Jahrhundert hineinreichen. Die Kollektion enthält unter anderem Bekleidung aus dem alten Ägypten, dem Nahen und Mittleren Osten, Rußland und den meisten europäischen Ländern. Sie veranschaulicht Unterschiede zwischen Regionen, Ständen (Königshäuser, Zivilstand, Militär, Adel und Klerus) und Modeströmungen, und umfaßt auch historische Trachten aus vielen asiatischen Ländern wie Persien, Indien, Birma (Myanmar), Thailand, Malaya, Indonesien, China und Japan.

Die Beschreibungen zu den Illustrationen beginnen auf Seite 209.

Histoire illustrée du costume

Dans cet ouvrage, les cinq cents illustrations en couleur datant du dix-neuvième siècle montrent les tenues des peuples dans diverses parties du monde et à différents stades de l'histoire. Ces gravures colorées à la main représentent des costumes remontant depuis l'âge de pierre jusqu'au dix-neuvième siècle. Cette collection contient entre autres des costumes de l'Egypte ancienne, du Moyen Orient, de la Russie et de la plupart des pays Européens, montrant les différences entre les régions, les classes – la royauté, les civils, les militaires, la noblesse, le clergé – et les styles en vogue. Les costumes historiques de nombreux pays asiatiques, incluant la Perse, l'Inde, la Birmanie, la Thailande, la Malaysie, l'Indonesie, la Chine et le Japon sont également représentés.

Les descriptions des illustrations peuvent être trouvées à partir de la page 209.

Storia illustrata del costume

Le cinquecento illustrazioni a colori contenute in questo libro risalgono al XIX secolo e mostrano capi d'abbigliamento utilizzati in diverse parti del mondo in vari periodi storici. Le incisioni, dipinte a mano, rappresentano abiti risalenti addirittura all'età della pietra e poi fino all'ottocento. Questa collezione raccoglie, tra altri, abiti provenienti dall'antico Egitto, dal medio oriente, dalla Russia e da gran parte dei paesi europei che illustrano le differenze regionali, stilistiche dell'epoca e di ceto sociale come ad esempio abiti regali, civili, militari, della nobiltá e della servitá. Costumi storici di molti paesi asiatici come Persia, India, Burma, Tailandia, Malesia, Indonesia, China e Giappone, sono anche rappresentati.

Le illustrazioni vengono descritte a pagina 209.

Historia illustrada del vestido

Las quinientas ilustraciones a todo color de esta obra, datadas del siglo XIX, muestran el atavío de los habitantes de distintas zonas del mundo en diversos períodos de la historia. A través de estos grabados ilustrados a mano se presentan trajes utilizados desde la Edad de Piedra hasta el siglo XIX.
La colección contiene prendas originarias del Egipto antiguo, Oriente Medio, Rusia y de la mayoría de países europeos, que muestran las diferencias entre regiones, clases (realeza, plebe, milicia, nobleza, clero...) y tendencias de la moda. También se incluye una descripción histórica de la indumentaria empleada en numerosos países asiáticos, entre ellos Persia, India, Birmania, Tailandia, Malaca, Indonesia, China y Japón.

Las ilustraciones se describen a partir de la página 209.

服裝史畫冊

本書內的 500 幅彩色插圖可追溯至十九世紀，一展世界各地的人們在不同歷史時期的服裝風采。手染彫版畫展示自石器時代直到十九世紀各時期的服裝。本書冊所收集的各色服裝中包括古埃及、中東、俄國、歐洲各國以及其他地區的服裝，區別展現不同區域、各社會階層（王族、平民、軍隊、貴族、教士）的服裝以及各種時裝款式。對許多亞洲國家的歷史服裝也給予了描繪，包括波斯、印度、緬甸、泰國、馬來亞、印度尼西亞、中國和日本。

自第 209 頁起有插圖説明。

絵で見る服装史

本書に収録された500点のカラーイラストは19世紀に作成されたもので、世界のいろいろな地域の人々の、様々な時代の服装を表しています。石器時代から19世紀に至るまでの服装を手染めの版画で紹介。本コレクションは古代エジプト、中東、ロシア、そしてヨーロッパのほとんど全ての国々の服装を網羅しており、地域、階級（王族や貴族、市民、軍隊、聖職者など）やファッションスタイルによる相違をご覧いただけます。さらに、ペルシャ、インド、ビルマ、タイ、マレー、インドネシア、中国、日本など、アジアの多数の国々の服装史も紹介しています。

イラストの解説は 209 ページからです。

Contents

33

162

List of illustrations

22
Top left: Young Byzantine nobleman
(left) and Byzantine emperor (right)
Top right: (from left to right) Byzantine
servant, Byzantine empress and
princess
Bottom left: Byzantine warrior (left)
and chancellor (right)
Bottom right: (from left to right)
Deacon, Byzantine bishop and Levite

23
Top left: Byzantines, early 6th century
Top right: Byzantines, early 6th century
Bottom left: Attendants of Byzantine
empress, mid-6th century
Bottom right: Byzantine emperor and
empress, 6th century

24
Frankish women and Emperor
Charlemagne, 8th century

25
Top left: Carolingians, 8th century
Top right: Carolingians, 8th century
Bottom left: Carolingians, 8th century
Bottom right: Carolingians, 8th century

26
Top left: Frankish king and queen,
8th century
Top right: Frankish noblewomen,
8th century
Bottom left: King Charles the Bald
(centre), 8th century
Bottom right: Emperor Henry II (left)
and Frankish bishop (right),
8th century

27
Top left: (from left to right) Monk,
bishop and priest, 11th century

Top right: Frankish king and queen,
11th century
Bottom left: Norman women (left and
centre) and noblewoman (right),
11th century
Bottom right: German noblewomen
(left and centre) and German
commoner's wife (right), 12th century

28
Crusaders, 11th century

29
Knights of the Order of St John
of Jerusalem, 11th or 12th century

30
Top left: German monarch with ladies,
13th century
Top right: German knight with his
family, 13th century
Bottom left: Italian scholars and
German lady (right), 13th century
Bottom right: (from left to right)
Knight, monarch and Templar,
13th century

31
Top left: Page and knight during
the 1st Crusade, 12th century
Top right: Ladies of the Order of
St John of Jerusalem, 12th or 13th
century
Bottom left: Crusaders, 12th or 13th
century
Bottom right: Templars, 12th or 13th
century

32
Top left: German lady with knight
in hunting costume, 14th century
Top right: Nobleman (left) and
commoner (right), 14th century

Bottom left: Noblewomen and English queen (right), 14th century
Bottom right: (from left to right) Monarch, page and nobleman, 14th century

33
Top left: Monarch (left) and knight (right), 14th century
Top right: Queen (left) and noblewoman (right), 14th century
Bottom left: Knight and lady, 14th century
Bottom right: German patricians, 14th century

34
Top left: England, first half of the 14th century
Top right: English commoners, second half of the 14th century
Bottom left: English merchants (left and centre) and nobleman (right), mid-14th century
Bottom right: English knights and lady, 14th century

35
Top left: Germany, 14th century
Top right: Germany, 14th century
Bottom left: Germany, 14th century
Bottom right: Germany, 14th century

36
Top left: (from left to right) Venetian admiral, young nobleman and Neapolitan knight, second half of the 14th century
Top right: Italian soldiers, second half of the 14th century
Bottom left: Italian women, second half of the 14th century
Bottom right: Young man (left),

Roman senator (2nd from the left) and Venetian nobleman (right), second half of the 14th century

37
Top left: Florentine ladies, first half of the 15th century
Top right: Florentine noblemen, first half of the 15th century
Bottom left: German ladies, first half of the 15th century
Bottom right: French noblemen, first half of the 15th century

38
Italy, 15th century

39
Top left: Italy, mid-14th century
Top right: Italy, 15th century
Bottom left: Italy, 15th century
Bottom right: Burgundians, second half of the 15th century

40
Ladies of the German court, 15th century

41
Top left: Members of the Burgundian court, first half of the 15th century
Top right: English royalty and nobility, 15th century
Bottom left: Germany, 15th century
Bottom right: Judge, commoner and peasant, 15th century

42
England, 15th century

43
France, 15th century

44
Top left: Germany, circa 1400
Top right: Germany, early 15th century
Bottom left: Germany, early 15th
century
Bottom right: Germany, mid-15th
century

45
Burgundians, mid-15th century

46
Top left: Burgundians, mid-15th
century
Top right: Burgundians, mid-15th
century
Bottom left: Burgundians, mid-15th
century
Bottom right: Burgundians, circa 1470

47
Top left: France, circa 1460-1480
Top right: France, circa 1460-1480
Bottom left: France, circa 1460-1480
Bottom right: France, circa 1460-1480

48
German patricians, second half of the
15th century

49
Top left: England, second half of the
15th century
Top right: France, second half of the
15th century
Bottom left: German patricians, second
half of the 15th century
Bottom right: France, second half of
the 15th century

50
Holland, circa 1470-1485

51
Top left: (from left to right)
Swiss standard-bearer, piper and
drummer, 15th century
Top right: (from left to right)
Swiss executioner, captain and boy,
15th century
Bottom left: Swiss soldiers,
15th century
Bottom right: Swiss soldiers,
15th century

52
German king and queen, first half
of the 16th century

53
Top left: German knight and
noblewoman, mid-15th century
Top right: German commoners,
first half of the 16th century
Bottom left: German knight and
noblewoman, second half of the
16th century
Bottom right: Burgundian soldiers,
circa 1470

54
German patrician ladies, first half
of the 16th century

55
Top left: French noblewoman followed
by her page, first half of the 16th
century
Top right: German magistrate (left)
and knight (right), first half of the
16th century
Bottom left: German patrician ladies,
first half of the 16th century
Bottom right: German lady and scholar,
first half of the 16th century

56
German patricians, early 16th century

57
Top left: German nobleman and lady, first half of the 16th century
Top right: German patricians, first half of the 16th century
Bottom left: German patricians, first half of the 16th century
Bottom right: German commoners, first half of the 16th century

58
German lansquenets, first half of the 16th century

59
Top left: Lansquenets, early 16th century
Top right: Drummer and standard-bearer, early 16th century
Bottom left: Piper and sergeant, early 16th century
Bottom right: Captain (left) and lieutenant (right), early 16th century

60
Top left: German lansquenets, first half of the 16th century
Top right: German hunters, first half of the 16th century
Bottom left: German lansquenets, first half of the 16th century
Bottom right: German peasants, first half of the 16th century

61
Top left: Germany, late 16th century
Top right: Germany, late 16th century
Bottom left: German merchant (left) and peasants, late 16th century
Bottom right: Germany, 16th century

62
From left to right: Frisians, late 16th century

63
Top left: Frisians, late 16th century
Top right: Frisians, North Sea coast, late 16th century
Bottom left: Frisians, late 16th century
Bottom right: German maid and driver, late 16th century

64
German commoners, first half of the 16th century

65
Top left: German noblewoman, 16th century
Top right: (from left to right) Horseman, cavalry general and lady, 16th century
Bottom left: French royals, 16th century
Bottom right: French royals, 16th century

66
Spanish and French royals, 16th century

67
Top left: Henry VIII and Anne of Cleves, 16th century
Top right: (from left to right) English merchant, nobleman and lady, 16th century
Bottom left: English royals, second half of the 16th century
Bottom right: French royals, second half of the 16th century

68
English royals, second half of the 16th century

69
German nobleman and lady, second half of the 16th century

70
Top left: German nobleman and lady, second half of the 16th century
Top right: Spanish nobleman and lady, second half of the 16th century
Bottom left: Members of the French court, second half of the 16th century
Bottom right: Members of the French court, second half of the 16th century

71
Top left: (from left to right) Chamberlain, cardinal and prelate, 16th or 17th century
Top right: (from left to right) Deacon, altar boy and subdeacon, 16th or 17th century
Bottom left: (from left to right) Guardsman, pope wearing robes and pope wearing domestic clothes, 16th or 17th century
Bottom right: Bishop in choir dress (left) and bishop in Mass robes, 16th or 17th century

72
Top left: Ladies from Rome (left) and Siena (right), 16th century
Top right: Ladies from Florence (left) and Padua (right), 16th century
Bottom left: Venetian senator and noblewomen, 16th century
Bottom right: Venetian Doge and his wife, 16th century

73
Top left: Neapolitans, late 16th century
Top right: Padua, late 16th century
Bottom left: Students from Padua (left

and centre) and peasant woman, late 16th century
Bottom right: Italy, late 16th century

74
Noblewomen from London, late 16th century

75
Dutch shipper's wife (left) and commoners, 16th or 17th century

76
Top left: German nobleman and lady, second half of the 16th century
Top right: French nobleman and lady, second half of the 16th century
Bottom left: (from left to right) Merchant's wife, servant and commoner's wife from London, late 16th century
Bottom right: (from left to right) Commoner's wife, lady, lord-mayor's wife and matron from London, mid-17th century

77
Top left: (from left to right) English merchant's wife, merchant and officer, 16th or 17th century
Top right: Women from Bohemia (left) and Spain (right), 16th or 17th century
Bottom left: (from left to right) Women from England, Paris, Rouen and Dieppe, 16th or 17th century
Bottom right: Poland, circa 1590-1660

78
Top left: Members of the Spanish court in the Netherlands, first half of the 17th century
Top right: Dutch commoner's wives, first half of the 17th century

Bottom left: Dutch artist (left) and young nobleman (right), first half of the 17th century
Bottom right: Dutch nobleman and lady, first half of the 17th century

79
Soldiers, first half of the 17th century

80
Top left: Men dressed in royal costume, first half of the 17th century
Top right: French noblemen, mid-17th century
Bottom left: Englishman and Fleming, mid-17th century
Bottom right: Noblemen, first half of the 17th century

81
Top left: German soldiers, first half of the 17th century
Top right: Soldiers, second half of the 17th century
Bottom left: German soldiers, second half of the 17th century
Bottom right: German soldiers, second half of the 17th century

82
French women in mourning, mid-17th century

83
French noblewomen, mid-17th century

84
Top left: Denmark, early 17th century
Top right: Norway, first half of the 17th century
Bottom left: Danish commoner's wife (left) and merchant (centre), first half of the 17th century

Bottom right: Denmark, first half of the 17th century

85
Top left: French cavalliers, second half of the 17th century
Top right: French cavalliers, second half of the 17th century
Bottom left: Commoners, first half of the 17th century
Bottom right: (from left to right) French peasant, commoner's wife and merchant, mid-17th century

86
Dutch commoners, second half of the 17th century

87
Top left: German nobleman and lady, second half of the 17th century
Top right: German nobleman and lady, second half of the 17th century
Bottom left: French nobleman and ladies, second half of the 17th century
Bottom right: French nobleman and lady, second half of the 17th century

88
Top left: French nobles in court dress, second half of the 17th century
Top right: Nobleman and lady, second half of the 17th century
Bottom left: French nobles in court dress, second half of the 17th century
Bottom right: Dutch nobleman and lady, second half of the 17th century

89
Top left: English nobles, mid-17th century
Top right: English nobles, mid-17th century

Bottom left: English nobles, second half of the 17th century
Bottom right: English nobles, first half of the 17th century

90
Top left: Women from Strasbourg (left and centre) and Basel (right), mid-17th century
Top right: (from left to right) Women from Munich, Nuremberg and Vienna, mid-17th century
Bottom left: (from left to right) Women from Frankfurt, the Palatinate and Swabia, Germany, mid-17th century
Bottom right: (from left to right) Servant, lady and matron from Cologne, mid-17th century

91
Top left: Switzerland, second half of the 17th century
Top right: Swiss peasants, second half of the 17th century
Bottom left: (from left to right) Swiss lady dressed to attend a church service, sergeant and courier, second half of the 17th century
Bottom right: (from left to right) Swiss lady in mourning, sergeant and mayor, second half of the 17th century

92
Mayor and town-councillor from Strasbourg, 17th century

93
Ladies from Strasbourg, 17th century

94
Crown princess of France and young nobleman, second half of the 17th century

95
Top left: Strasbourg, second half of the 17th century
Top right: Duchess and palace guard, early 18th century
Bottom left: Noble ladies, circa 1700
Bottom right: Noble ladies and palace guard, second half of the 17th century

96
Top left: Ladies from Strasbourg, second half of the 17th century
Top right: Swiss ladies, early 18th century
Bottom left: Swiss ladies, early 18th century
Bottom right: Swiss peasants, early 18th century

97
Top left: French abbott and noblewoman, early 18th century
Top right: (from left to right) Swiss student, gentleman and town councillor, early 18th century
Bottom left: German lady and gentleman, first half of the 18th century
Bottom right: French lady and gentleman, first half of the 18th century

98
Members of the French court, first half of the 18th century

99
Top left: Officer (left) and musketeer (right) of the French guards, first half of the 18th century
Top right: French officers, first half of the 18th century
Bottom left: French peasants (left and centre) and country constable (right), first half of the 18th century

Bottom right: French nobleman (left) and officer (right), first half of the 18th century

100
Top left: French marshal and attending officers, early 18th century
Top right: Louis xv and French general, early 18th century
Bottom left: Austrian cavalry, early 18th century
Bottom right: Austrian infantry, early 18th century

101
Austrian general and officer, second half of the 18th century

102
Top left: (from left to right) German grenadier, cuirassier and general, circa 1730
Top right: (from left to right) German soldier, officer, drummer and sergeant, first half of the 18th century
Bottom left: (from left to right) Grenadiers, dragoon and infantryman, first half of the 18th century
Bottom right: Austrian soldiers, first half of the 18th century

103
Top left: (from left to right) Prussian officer and grenadier, circa 1770
Top right: (from left to right) Officer, curassier and grenadier, circa 1770
Bottom left: (from left to right) French generals, circa 1800
Bottom right: France, late 18th century

104
Austrian hussar (left) and infantryman (right), second half of the 18th century

105
Top left: France, late 18th century
Top right: French infantrymen, late 18th century
Bottom left: (from left to right) French hussar, cavalryman and infantryman, late 18th century
Bottom right: (from left to right) French general and officers, late 18th century

106
Top left: Benedictine monks
Top right: Franciscan monks
Bottom left: Hyronimite monk (hermit)
Bottom right: Capuchin monks

107
Top left: Capuchin nuns, late 18th century
Top right: Dominican nuns, late 18th century
Bottom left: Benedictine nuns, late 18th century
Bottom right: Ursuline nuns, late 18th century

108
Abbott and female servant, second half of the 18th century

109
Lady wearing a crinoline, second half of the 18th century

110
Lady and gentleman, circa 1780

111
French ladies, circa 1775-1780

112
Top left: Lady and gentleman, circa 1775

Top right: French lady and gentleman,
circa 1780
Bottom left: French ladies and
gentleman, circa 1775-1780
Bottom right: French ladies and
gentleman, circa 1780-1785

113
French ladies, circa 1790

114
Top left: Women from Mannheim (left)
and Strasbourg (centre and right),
circa 1770-1790
Top right: (from left to right) Women
from Karlsruhe, Vienna and Frankfurt,
circa 1770-1790
Bottom left: Women from Augsburg,
Germany, circa 1770-1790
Bottom right: Women from Bavaria,
Germany, circa 1770-1790

115
Germany, circa 1790

116
Top left: France, circa 1795
Top right: Germany, circa 1790
Bottom left: French bourgeoisie,
circa 1790
Bottom right: Germany, circa 1790

117
Top left: Germany, circa 1785
Top right: Germany, circa 1800
Bottom left: Germany, circa 1795
Bottom right: Germany, circa 1795

118
France, circa 1795

119
Germany, circa 1800

120
Western Europe, circa 1800-1810

121
Western Europe, circa 1800-1810

122
Western Europe, circa 1800-1810

123
Germany and France, circa 1810

124
Germany and France, circa 1810

125
Western Europe, circa 1820

126
Germany and France, circa 1805

127
Top left: Germany, after 1800
Top right: Western Europe,
circa 1800-1810
Bottom left: Western Europe,
circa 1820
Bottom right: Germany and France,
circa 1805

128
Western Europe, circa 1815

129
Top left: Western Europe, circa 1820
Top right: Germany, circa 1825-1830
Bottom left: Germany, circa 1825-1830
Bottom right: Waitress and middle-class
family from Munich, Germany, circa
1820

130
Germany, circa 1825-1830

131
Top left: Bavarian military, circa
1810-1825
Top right: Bavarian military, circa
1805-1825
Bottom left: Bavarian military, circa
1815-1825
Bottom right: Bavarian military, circa
1810-1825

132
Top left: The Netherlands,
19th century
Top right: The Netherlands,
19th century
Bottom left: The Netherlands,
19th century
Bottom right: The Netherlands,
19th century

133
Top left: Man and woman from
Scheveningen, the Netherlands,
19th century
Top right: Women from Frisia,
the Netherlands, 19th century
Bottom left: Man and woman from
Marken, the Netherlands, 19th century
Bottom right: Men from Marken,
the Netherlands, 19th century

134
Top left: Man and woman from
Hamburg (left and centre) and woman
from Hannover (right), Germany,
19th century
Top right: Man and women from
Schleswig-Holstein, Germany, 19th
century
Bottom left: Man and women from
Frisia, Germany, 19th century
Bottom right: Women from Frisia,
Germany, 19th century

135
Top left: Men from Bavaria, Germany,
19th century
Top right: Women from Bavaria,
Germany, 19th century
Bottom left: Women from Bavaria,
Germany, 19th century
Bottom right: Man and woman from
Bavaria, Germany, 19th century

136
Top left: Men from Baden, Germany,
19th century
Top right: Women from Baden,
Germany, 19th century
Bottom left: Women from Baden,
Germany, 19th century
Bottom right: Woman and men from
Baden, Germany, 19th century

137
Top left: Man and women from Baden,
Germany, 19th century
Top right: Man and women from
Baden, Germany, 19th century
Bottom left: Women and child from
Baden, Germany, 19th century
Bottom right: Women and man from
Baden, Germany, 19th century

138
Top left: Woman and man from Baden,
Germany, 19th century
Top right: Man and women from
Baden, Germany, 19th century
Bottom left: Woman and men from
Baden, Germany, 19th century
Bottom right: Man and women from
Baden, Germany, 19th century

139
Top left: Man and women from Alsace,
France, 19th century

Top right: Man and women from
Alsace, France, 19th century
Bottom left: Man and women from
Alsace, France, 19th century
Bottom right: Women from Alsace,
France, 19th century

140
Man and women from Brittany,
France, 19th century

141
Man and women from Brittany,
France, 19th century

142
Man and woman from Brittany,
France, 19th century

143
Man and woman from Tyrol,
19th century

144
Men from Tyrol, 19th century

145
Top left: Women from Bavaria,
Germany, 19th century
Top right: Women from Bavaria,
Germany, 19th century
Bottom left: Women from Bavaria,
Germany, 19th century
Bottom right: Men from Bavaria,
Germany, 19th century

146
Top left: Woman and men from Tyrol,
19th century
Top right: Man and women from Tyrol,
19th century
Bottom left: Man and women from
Tyrol, 19th century

Bottom right: Man and women from
Tyrol, 19th century

147
Top left: Man and woman from Tyrol,
19th century
Top right: Men and woman from Tyrol,
19th century
Bottom left: Women from Tyrol, 19th
century
Bottom right: Woman and men from
Tyrol, 19th century

148
Top left: Women from Bern,
Switzerland, 19th century
Top right: Women from Wallis,
Switzerland, 19th century
Bottom left: Women from Zug,
Switzerland, 19th century
Bottom right: Women from St. Gallen,
Switzerland, 19th century

149
Top left: Women from Tyrol,
19th century
Top right: Men and woman from
Aargau, Switzerland, late 18th century
Bottom left: Men and woman from
Aargau and St. Gallen, Switzerland,
late 18th century
Bottom right: Man and women from
Bern, Switzerland, late 18th century

150
Switzerland, late 18th century

151
Switzerland, late 18th century

152
Top left: Switzerland, late 18th century
Top right: Man and woman from

Lucerne, Switzerland, late 18th century
Bottom left: Man and woman from
Freiburg, Switzerland, late 18th century
Bottom right: Man and women from
Schaffhausen (left and centre) and
Appenzell (right), Switzerland, late
18th century

153
Top left: Men from Valencia (left) and
Granada (right), Spain, 19th century
Top right: Alicante and Zamora, Spain,
19th century
Bottom left: Man from Leon (left) and
couple from Segovia (centre and left),
Spain, 19th century
Bottom right: Man and women from
Murcia, Spain, 19th century

154
Top left: Italy, 19th century
Top right: Italy, 19th century
Bottom left: Italy, 19th century
Bottom right: Italy, 19th century

155
Top left: Woman and men from
Dalmatia, 19th century
Top right: Men and women from
Dalmatia, 19th century
Bottom left: Women from Dalmatia,
19th century
Bottom right: Man and women from
Dalmatia, 19th century

156
Polish or Russian horsemen,
16th century

157
Russian (left) and Polish (right)
noblemen, 16th century

158
Russian women dressed in winter
costume, 17th or 18th century

159
Boyars, Russia, 17th or 18th century

160
Top left: Polish lady and Russian
nobleman, 16th century
Top right: Polish nobility, 16th century
Bottom left: Tsar (centre) and Boyars,
Russia, 17th or 18th century
Bottom right: Russia, 17th or 18th
century

161
Top left: Caucasus, 19th century
Top right: Russia, 19th century
Bottom left: Russia, 19th century
Bottom right: Russia, 19th century

162
Russia, 19th century

163
Top left: Caucasus, 19th century
Top right: Central Europe,
19th century
Bottom left: Central Europe,
19th century
Bottom right: Central Europe,
19th century

164
Bulgaria, 19th century

165
Central Europe, 19th century

166
Central Europe, 19th century

167
Top left: Ottoman women
Top right: Ottoman Empire, 17th or
18th century
Bottom left: Ottoman pasha (centre)
and noblemen
Bottom right: Ottoman soldiers, 17th or
18th century

168
Ottoman soldiers, 17th or 18th century

169
Top left: Janissaries, Ottoman Empire,
17th or 18th century
Top right: Prince from Lebanon (left)
and man from Damascus (right),
19th century
Bottom left: Armenian girl (left),
Drusian man (centre) and man from
Damascus (right), 19th century
Bottom right: (from left to right)
Dervish, Syrian man, Drusian woman
and man from Damascus, 19th century

170
From left to right: Man and woman
from Syria and man from Baghdad,
Iraq, 19th century

171
Top left: Egypt, 19th century
Top right: Egypt, 19th century
Bottom left: Egypt, 19th century
Bottom right: Egypt, 19th century

172
Women from the region of Damascus,
Syria, 19th century

173
Top left: Lebanon, 19th century
Top right: King of Delhi (front left) and

Brahman student (front right), India,
19th century
Bottom left: Woman from Tomsk (left),
Kirgiz woman and man (centre and
right), 19th century
Bottom right: Bashirs from Turkmen-
istan and Tartar woman from Kasan,
Uzbekistan (right), 19th century

174
Central Asia, 19th century

175
Tartar woman from Siberia (left) and
Kalmuck woman and man (centre and
right), 19th century

176
Nomads from Amur, Heilongjiang,
China, 19th century

177
Dervish (left) and Turkoman woman,
19th century

178
Afghanistan, 19th century

179
Afghanistan, 19th century

180
Top left: Women and man from
Turkestan, 19th century
Top right: Afghans from the Khyber
Pass, 19th century
Bottom left: (from left to right)
Man from Khiwa, emir of
Bukhara,Turkoman, girl from
Samarkand and man from Bukhara,
Uzbekistan, 19th century
Bottom right: Men from Khiva,
Uzbekistan, 19th century

181
Tibetan women, 19th century

182
Top left: Indian dancer (left) and
Afghan men, 19th century
top right: Tibetan women and priest
(right), 19th century
Bottom left: Men from Kashmir,
19th century
Bottom right: (from left to right)
Dancer, lifeguard and maharaja of
Kashmir, 19th century

183
Indian monarch with his wife and
child and a Hindu woman (right),
19th century

184
South Indian Hindus in Malaya,
19th century

185
South Indian Muslims in Malaya,
19th century

186
Parsi from Singapore and Bombay,
19th century

187
Sinhalese, Sri Lanka, 19th century

188
Sinhalese, Sri Lanka, 19th century

189
Sinhalese, Sri Lanka, 19th century

190
Sinhalese dancers, Sri Lanka,
19th century

191
Priests from Yunnan, China,
19th century

192
Nobleman and girls from Yunnan,
China, 19th century

193
Tonkin, Vietnam, 19th century

194
From left to right: Burmese officer,
minister in gala dress and girl from
Mandalay, 19th century

195
Women and children of the Karen
tribe, Burma, 19th century

196
Burma, 19th century

197
Burma, 19th century

198
Buddhist monk (left), king and queen
of Siam (Thailand), 19th century

199
Top left: Actresses from Jaffna,
Sri Lanka, 19th century
Top right: Actors from Jaffna, Sri Lanka,
19th century
Bottom left: Actors and actresses from
Java, 19th century
Bottom right: Actors and actresses from
Thailand, 19th century

200
Regent of Cirebon (left) and man from
Nias, Indonesia, 19th century

201
From left to right: Minangkabau and
Bataks from Sumatra and man from
Makasar (Ujung Pandang), Sulawesi,
Indonesia, 19th century

202
Dayak men and a princess from
Borneo, Indonesia, 19th century

203
From left to right: Dayak woman,
Dayak warrior and noblewoman from
Borneo, Indonesia, 19th century

204
Chinese actresses, 19th century

205
Chinese babas from the Straits
settlements (left and centre) and
Chinese shoemaker from Singapore,
19th century

206
Merchant from Penang, Malaysia and
Chinese woman from Macao,
19th century

207
Chinese (Hokkien) bearer (left) and
merchant (right) from Penang,
Malaysia, 19th century

208
Top left: Japanese soldiers,
19th century
Top right: Japanese commoners,
19th century
Bottom left: Japan, 19th century
Bottom right: Japanese women and
child, 19th century